A CRITICAL STUDY

of

THE SOURCES OF

THE HISTORY OF THE EMPEROR NERO

by

John Nicholas Henry Jahn, Ph.D.

Submitted

in partial fulfillment of the requirements for the degree of

DOCTOR OF PHILOSOPHY

at

NEW YORK UNIVERSITY

May, 1920

In the interest of creating a more extensive selection of rare historical book reprints, we have chosen to reproduce this title even though it may possibly have occasional imperfections such as missing and blurred pages, missing text, poor pictures, markings, dark backgrounds and other reproduction issues beyond our control. Because this work is culturally important, we have made it available as a part of our commitment to protecting, preserving and promoting the world's literature. Thank you for your understanding.

To

DOCTOR ERNEST GOTTLIEB SIHLER

Professor of the Latin Language and Literature
in the New York University

The Eminent Scholar and Teacher

and to

JULIA GERTRUDE JAHN

My Faithful Wife

This Little Book Is Gratefully Inscribed

CONTENTS

Introduction	5
The Annals of Tacitus	7
The Life of Nero by Suetonius	20
The History of Nero by Dio Cassius	27
Inscriptions	38
Coins	39
Bibliography	43

Introduction

Our sources of the history of Nero and his reign are not very numerous.

Fortunately, we have the works of three of the historians who wrote on this period at a time that was not so remote as to render their records of little value. (Chapters XII-XVI of the Annals of Tacitus (c.55-120 A. D.) cover the reign of Nero to the year 66 A. D., including his relation to Claudius during the last years of that emperor, and are so far complete. The Life of Nero by Suetonius (c.75-160 A. D.) has come down to us entire. Of the History of Nero by Dio Cassius (born 155 A. D.) in his Roman History, Books 61-63, we have only the abridgment of Xiphilinus and the extracts of Zonaras. Xiphilinus was a monk of the eleventh century who at the request of Michael VII (1071-78) wrote an epitome of Books 36-80 of the History of Dio Cassius, the last twenty of which would otherwise have been lost. Considering Dio's mode of writing, we are inclined to think that by the abridgment not much of the substance of the original work has beeen lost.[1] Moreover, the work of Johannes Zonaras, a Byzantine historian of the middle of the twelfth century, in his Epitome of History (from creation to 1118 A. D.), as far as the history of Nero and other Roman emperors is concerned, consists in the main of excerpts from Dio, and thus he supplies in the passages that can be recognized as such, some of the parts that are lacking in the abridgment of Xiphilinus.

There are but a few other sources, and these are all quite meager, as far at least as the history of the emperor is concerned. A few fragments of early Roman historians remain.[2] A small number of inscriptions has been preserved,[3] and a larger number of Roman and other coins of that period.[4] The work of Josephus (b. 37 A. D.) on the Antiquities of the Jews extends to the twelfth year of Nero's reign; but it is, in the first place, a history of the Jewish people, and then the work was written by the Flavian courtier with the intention to create among the Greeks and Romans a higher opinion of his despised people,[5] and, on the other hand, the author was profuse in the flattery of his patrons,[6] among whom Poppaea, the wife of Nero, had been, and whenever there was an occasion to flatter he was not much concerned about the truth.[7] Eusebius of Caesarea (died 340

---

[1] Sandys, Hist. of Lat. Scholarship I, 117.
[2] Peter, Historicorum Rom. Fragmenta.
[3] Jani Gruteri Inscriptiones Antiquae.
[4] Joseph Eckhel, Doctrina Nuinorum Veterum.
[5] Pauly, Real-encl. d. kl. Altert., Josephus.
[6] Cp. the concluding remark in his Autobiography, Ch. 76.
[7] Peter, Die gesch. Lit., I, 398.

A. D.) supplies information on the history of the Christian Church under Nero,[1] especially on the first imperial persecution of the Christians.[2] The History of Orosius, a Spanish priest, who about 414 A. D. went to Hippo and by Augustine was assigned the task of supplementing the "City of God" by a review of history for the purpose of disproving the pagan assertion that the fall of Rome was a consequence of her abandonment of the old religion of the state, has little or no value as a source of the history of Nero, which is touched upon in the last of the seven books of the work. For he generally handles the facts in an arbitrary and uncritical way to suit his theological purpose,[3] accepting mere legend as though it were authentic history.[4]

A study of the sources of the history of Nero must therefore in the main be limited to the works of Tacitus, Suetonius, and Dio Cassius.

While it is not altogether futile to attempt to determine what sources these writers again used when composing their works, and to investigate to what extent they used them,[5] it is vastly more profitable to the student of history to carefully compare the records of these writers with each other and with the few other sources that have come down to us. With due consideration of the author's character and life, his method, and the connection in which his statements appear, such a comparison will afford a fairly safe basis for correct judgments on the conditions and events which they record.

The writer believed himself justified in omitting almost entirely from the present study such authors as did not write directly on Nero and his reign, but from whose works nevertheless material of some importance might be gathered, as Seneca, Pliny the Elder, Plutarch (Life of Galba), Martial, Statius, Lucan, Persius, and Petronius, and the Christian writers.

---

[1] Euseb., Hist. eccl. 2, 20. seq.
[2] 2, 25.
[3] Sam. Dill, Roman Society, p. 66 seq.
[4] Cp. Orosius 15, 4. The exploits of the Amazons.
[5] O. Clason, Tac. und Suet., eine vergleichende Untersuchung mit Ruecksicht auf die beiderseitigen Quellen. Jan Bergmans, Die Quellen der Vita Tiberii des Cassius Dio.

Tacitus

With regard to Tacitus, the earliest of our literary sources of the history of Nero, opposite views have prevailed among scholars.

Prof. Wilkins has given the view of the one side as follows: "As a historian Tacitus cannot be considered impartial. The story of the reign of Tiberius, Claudius, and Nero is told throughout from a standpoint of bitter hostility. Not that Tacitus is often consciously unfair. But the coloring which he gives to his facts, and especially the suggestion of motives in which he indulges, show the satirist rather than the historian. The emperors are to him mainly the enemies of the senate, in which he fancied he could find what still remained of old Roman freedom and virtue. Their undoubted services to the cause of peace and good government throughout the civilized world are lightly touched; every instance of jealousy and caprice in dealing with the nobles of the capitol is dwelt upon. Often the sources from which he drew his accounts are suspicious; and he shows but little critical faculty in testing them. The desire for effect leads him to paint his picture of men and things in colors far too glaring and sharply contrasted to be true to nature. He lived in an age of satire; and the last thing that we expect from a satirist, saddened by his own experience of life, is a fair and well-balanced judgment."[1]

Nipperdey, summarizing the view of the opposite side, says of this criticism: "Diesen Angriffen kann nur zum ausserst geringen Teil—eine Berechtigung zugestanden werden—; sie beruhen fast durchaus nicht auf klaren festen Beweisen, wie sie die Sache erfordert, sondern auf willkuerlichen Annahmen und subjektivem Ermessen, zum nicht geringen Teil auf Irrtuemern und Entstellungen, auf einer Voreingenommenheit, welche selbst das am naechsten Liegende und Einfachste nicht erkennen laesst."[2]

When eminent scholars disagree, an attempt to form an independent judgment, however humble, will appear the more fully justified.

The Sources of Tacitus

In his history of the emperor Nero, Tacitus refers to and quotes from *numerous sources*.

There are references like these: adnotant seniores, tradunt plerique scriptores, sunt qui tradiderint, sunt qui abnuant, plures

[1] A. S. Wilkins, Rom. Lit. p. 126.
[2] C. Tacitus, Einl. p. 31.

asseverabant, auctores prodidere, tradidere quidam, quidam scriptores.[1] It is, of course, a question whether all of these expressions refer to writers; but very likely they do, since Ann. 14, 2. the distinction is made between the writers named, other writers, and tradition (fama). The remark of Tacitus in his history of Augustus, made twice, that he had recourse to sources which other writers had overlooked,[2] shows that he made the most extensive use of the works of others.

Seldom does he mention any historians by name. In the history of Nero mention is made of Fabius Rusticus, Pliny the Elder, and Cluvius;[3] then Fabius and Cluvius are mentioned together;[4] then Domitius Corbulo, Pliny the Elder, and Fabius are mentioned singly.[5]

Fabius Rusticus was an older contemporary of Tacitus,[6] who ranks him with Livy, calling him "recentium eloquentissimus auctor."[7] He was a friend of Seneca, to whose patronage he owed much.[8]

Cluvius Rufus was also an older contemporary of Tacitus, as he had already been consul under Galigula.[9] He announced Nero's first public appearance as a singer in Rome,[10] and if Dio is not mistaken, he served the emperor in the same capacity on his tour in Greece in the year 67.[11] This would go to show that Cluvius enjoyed the favor of Nero almost to the end of his reign, and very likely never lost it. Tacitus calls him "facundus et pacis artibus, bellis inexpertus."[12] He was considered a historian of first rank. Pliny praises his impartiality,[13] and Tacitus ranks him with or above Fabius Rusticus.[14]

Pliny the Elder (23-79 A. D.) continued the history of Aufidius Bassus. In this work was included the time of Nero.[15] His trustworthiness in determining the facts[16] is generally admitted.

That Tacitus used the works of these three historians above others when writing the history of Nero, is apparent from the fact that more than once he records their divergent statements.

[1] Ann. 13, 3; 13, 17; 14. 19; 14, 51; 15, 38; 15, 45; 16, 6.
[2] Ann. 4, 53; 6.7.
[3] Ann. 13, 20.
[4] Ann. 14, 2.
[5] Ann. 15, 16; 15, 53; 15, 61.
[6] Ann. 13, 20.
[7] Agr. 10.
[8] Ann. 13, 20.
[9] Josephus, Antiq. 19, 1, 13.
[10] Suet. Ner. 21.
[11] Dio C. 63. 20.
[12] Hist. 1, 9.
[13] Ep. 9, 19, 5.
[14] Ann. 13, 20; 14, 2.
[15] Plin. n. h., praef. 20.
[16] Plin. ep. 5, 8, 5.

Cn. Domitius Corbulo wrote memoirs on the Armenian war (55-63 A. D.), which he conducted. The elder Pliny refers to this work several times in his Natural History.[1] It was at least first-hand information.

Besides the works of these historians Tacitus consulted various documents, such as the journals of the senate[2] and those of the City,[3] the decrees of the emperor, and the records of the courts. The "publica acta" referred to Ann. 12, 24. Nipperdey takes to be inscriptions. Documents that were being preserved in the imperial archives are not mentioned; it may be assumed that Tacitus had no access to these.

Use of Sources

The Principle of Consensus

How did Tacitus use his sources? He has himself stated his method. "We shall follow the consensus of authors, and where they differ, we shall relate what each records under his name."[4] The word "auctorum" has caused some difficulty. Does he mean all the authors? How then can we explain that in several instances he introduces divergent opinions with a mere "quidam," "sunt qui," etc.? In fact, in books 13-16 only Corbulo is mentioned as an authority besides Fabius, Cluvius, and Pliny. It has therefore been suggested that "horum" has been omitted before "auctorum."[5] This would be a simple solution; but it seems too radical. Could a citation introduced by "quidam," etc., not also be said to be, in a sense, "sub nominibus ipsorum" (nomine ipsorum)? The use of the phrase in this sense would, we must admit, be unusual;[6] but it is not impossible.[7]

If we may take it in this sense, Tacitus means to say that in case his sources differ he will not record the one view only which to him seems the correct one, thus making a statement on his own authority, but that he will state the different views; if the historians are well known, he will mention their names, otherwise he will refer to them in an indefinite way.

However that may be, Tacitus was guided in the use of his sources by the consensus of the authors, at least as far as the history of Nero is concerned.[8] It may seem strange, even though we limit the use of this principle to the history of Nero, that it was not stated before. But the historians of antiquity did

[1] 2, 180; 5, 83; 6, 23.
[2] Ann. 15, 74.
[3] Ann. 3, 3.
[4] Ann. 13, 20.
[5] Nipperdey, Einl. p. 21.
[6] Cf. A. Draeger, Ueber Syntax u. Stil d. Tac.
[7] Ann. 13, 25: sub nomine Neronis.
[8] Cp. Ann. 14, 9: Haec consensu produntur.

not preface their works with a chapter on the principles and methods of historiography. Remarks on this subject must be expected to have been made by the way, when an occasion called for an explanation of the author's view. This is the first occasion of the kind in the history of Nero to which the principle clearly applies.

Tacitus then did not use the method attributed to some other ancient historians, to follow in the main one author and to use all the other works at his disposal as secondary sources for the purpose of supplementing or correcting. For this reason he must be ranked higher than some other ancient historians.

Clason[1] has attempted to prove that Tacitus after all followed the customary method with regard to the use of his sources, with this difference only that he based his work on three sources, Fabius, Cluvius, and Pliny—a triune source he calls it —instead of one. But would this not practically amount to the modern method? Strange that the very first example adduced by Clason to support his theory[2] shows that other sources received considerable attention, while Pliny is not even mentioned. Clason does not hesitate to say that Pliny's name must here be understood as associated with that of Cluvius, and elsewhere[3] he would even have it associated with the unnamed Cluvius.[4] This will, of course, not do.

We have every reason to believe that Tacitus based his history of Nero on the works of all the earlier writers who had recorded the history of that period. This, together with the fact that he was their contemporary and wrote not many years after their works had been published, and at a time when data on which they disagreed could easily be investigated, lends much authority to the work of Tacitus.

Critical Use of Sources

Nor was Tacitus uncritical in the use of these sources.

Fabius, Pliny, and Cluvius disagree on *the dismissal of Burrus* and his subsequent retention in office upon the request of Seneca.[5] Tacitus here not only considers the consensus of Pliny and Cluvius over against Fabius, but is inclined to disbelieve Fabius because of his relation to Seneca, to whose favor Fabius owed his position.[6]

[1] Clason, Tacitus und Sueton, p. 11.
[2] Ann. 14, 2.
[3] 15, 61.
[4] Clason, Tac. u. Suet. p. 14.
[5] Ann. 13, 20.
[6] Sane Fabius inclinat ad laudes Senecae, cuius amicitia floruit.

Again, Tacitus rejects the testimony of Fabius in regard to the *incestuous approaches between Nero and Agrippina*. While Fabius ascribes them to Nero's passion, Cluvius says they were a part of Agrippina's plan to regain her former influence over the prince, and with him the other writers agree and to this view tradition inclines.[1]

The third instance in which Fabius is named regards the *death of Seneca*.[2] Tacitus says that according to Fabius the tribune sent to announce to Seneca his doom hesitated to execute the emperor's command, and, in order to avoid a meeting with Seneca, sent a centurion to apprise him of Nero's will. Fabius, on account of his friendship to Seneca, might indeed be supposed to have gathered reliable information on the great philosopher's death;[3] but must he not again be suspected of being partial to Seneca in portraying that "want of spirit" which was found in all but Seneca and a few others? However, as there are no divergent reports on this point to confirm the suspicion, Tacitus abstains from uttering it, merely citing Fabius on the incident and withholding his own judgment.

The same critical use he made of *Pliny*. In 13, 12. Pliny's testimony is accepted, because it agrees with Cluvius and the preponderance of tradition.

Then Pliny is cited as relating that, after Nero would have been killed, *Piso*, according to *the plan of the conspirators*, was to be led to the Praetorian camp attended by Antonia, the daughter of Claudius Caesar, to gain the favor of the people. There was evidently no other report to confirm this. Tacitus therefore, judging it on its own merits finds it improbable, because Antonia would hardly have lent her name and risked her life in a project that held out no hope to her, and because Piso, known for his affection for his wife, would not have entered into matrimony with another woman.[4]

Whether Tacitus in the history of Nero used *Cluvius* more extensively than other sources,[5] cannot be ascertained. It is true, he does not criticise him, as he criticises Fabius and Pliny; but it must be noted that he mentions him only twice,[6] and that in both instances Cluvius happens to have the consensus of others. There was no occasion for criticism.

How the *unnamed authors* were used is indicated Ann. 14, 59. Tacitus is here relating the murder of Rubellius Plautus in Asia, whose assassins found him in the middle of the day engaged in

[1] Ann. 14, 2.
[2] 15, 61.
[3] Clason, Tac. u. Suet. p. 15.
[4] Ann. 15, 53.
[5] Clason, Tac. u. Suet. p. 15.
[6] 13, 20; 14, 2.

bodily exercises. After mentioning a number of possible reasons for this lack of resistance, he says: "Certain it is that the assassins found him," etc. In this case the reports varied so much, that whatever consensus remained was negligible. Tacitus therefore mentions the various opinions on the point of difference without passing any judgment, and then records the undisputed fact of the murder.

In a similar way he states that according to some authors *Nero ordered Seneca to be poisoned* in 64 A. D. He does not argue from the silence of other authors—perhaps the majority—to the truth of the report of a few, but lets the reader judge himself, if he will.[1]

He also refrains from judging in cases in which the weight of the testimony for and of that against the truth of a statement are equal, or nearly so. After having described the assassination of Agrippina, he says: "In these particulars authors are agreed, but as to *whether Nero viewed the breathless body of his mother* and praised its beauty, there are those who have affirmed it, and those who deny it."[2]

Another instance concerns the *death of Poppaea*. Some attribute her death to a kick that Nero gave her when she was pregnant; others say that he poisoned her. This Tacitus can not believe, as Nero desired to have children and was devoted to his wife, and he censures the latter authors for having written from spite rather than conviction.[3]

Tacitus then, though generally following the consensus of the historians, is critical in their use, considering both the character of the authors and the circumstances of their life, and the agreement of their reports with established facts.

Influence of a Gloomy and Fatalistic View

The influence which his gloomy and fatalistic view of his time had upon Tacitus' presentation of the history of Nero *must not be overrated*. It is there, to be sure. Tacitus had lived the years of his childhood under Nero and had been mature enough in 68-70 to be deeply impressed with the downfall of the tyrant and the violence and bloodshed which marked the rise and fall of the three emperors. The following years, the happy reign of Vespasian and Titus (70-81), during which he grew into manhood and entered the senate, had not wiped out this impression, when the bloodthirsty Domitian began to reign (—96 A. D.),

[1] Ann. 15. 64.
[2] 14. 9.
[3] 16. 6.

who, like Nero, sought to destroy the senate.[1] Tacitus lived to see the rule of better men, Nerva, Trajan, and Hadrian. And this was the time in which he wrote his history of the Roman emperors, the Annals being published in 116 or 117 A. D.[2] But he had not freed his mind entirely from the obsession of that pessimistic view of the Roman world. As he looks back, he still sees "the wrath of heaven against the Roman state."[3] This view could not fail to influence his presentation of events in his historical works and, of course, was very strong in his history of Nero, the horrors of whose reign he had seen repeated under Domitian.[4]

The influence of this view is noticed chiefly in his choice of material. Although his principal object in writing the Annals was "ne virtutes sileantur,"[5] the dark colors prevail in the picture he draws both of Nero and of that time, and thus he overdraws, as a comparison with Suetonius will show. "Not the Histories only," says Merivale, "but all the other works of Tacitus, are drawn up almost in the form of indictments against his own age."[6]

Fairness

On the other hand, Tacitus strives to be fair. He does not want to put the worst construction on every thing, the proneness of people to do which he deplores.[7]

He seems bitter and unfair in his contemptuous words on the composition of Nero's poems and on his dabbling with philosophy.[8] Poets, he says, who were invited to Nero's table patched their lines to the emperor's crude effusions. His only proof for the truth of this assertion is the lack of inspiration and uniformity that the poems show. To the squabbles of philosophers of opposite views Nero listened, says Tacitus, only for amusement. But there was hardly any need of proof in these instances. It was well known that at least Nero's letters to the senate were written by Seneca, and it is apparent that there could be no philosophy for a character like Nero's; he could have no real interest in a contest of philosophers of different schools.

The speech to Nero, in which Seneca asks leave to retire from public life and to return his wealth to Nero, and Nero's reply,

[1] On Domitian's reign cp. Tac. Agr. 3, 10 ff (Tot annis, quibus invenes ad senectutem, senes prope ed ipsos exactae terminos per silentium venimus.)
[2] Nipperdey. C. Tac., Einl. p. 11.
[3] Ann. 16, 16.
[4] Cf. Agr. 45: Nero tamen subtraxit oculos suos lussitque scelera, non spectavit: praecipua sub Domitiano miseriarum pars erat videre et aspici, etc.
[5] Ann. 3, 65.
[6] Hist. of the Rom., 7, 210.
[7] Ann. 15, 6. 4.
[8] 14, 16.

may seem invented for the defense of the admired philosopher. But is it not possible that the speech was recorded by Seneca himself and left among his writings together with a reproduction of Nero's reply?[1] In this case it would have been Seneca who had been partial to himself.

However that may be, Tacitus is *a lover of truth;* he seeks to ascertain the truth and to present it without partiality; and, on the whole, he certainly succeeds in doing so.

In the same paragraph in which he states that Nero acquired the empire by crime, he says that the proconsul I. Silanus was killed without Nero's knowledge, at the order of Agrippina, and that Narcissus, the freedman of Claudius, was driven to death by Agrippina against Nero's will.[2] However much Tacitus abhors the tyrant, however severe his judgments upon Nero may be, when they seem justified, he frequently rejects testimony that is adverse to the emperor. He will not accept the testimony of Fabius that the attempts at incest between Nero and his mother proceeded from the prince;[3] and he cannot believe that Nero poisoned Poppaea, as some have stated.[4] Other examples could be added.

The passage on the *persecution of the Christians* under Nero[5] has been the occasion of much criticism. Tacitus is said to have erred both with regard to the extent and duration of the persecution, and the accusation brought against the Christians.

He says that a *vast multitude* was killed. This phrase alone, Ramsay[6] points out, might well be interpreted, in a writer like Tacitus, as indicating that the number arrested and tried was great in view of the charge, viz. incendiarism, in which, as a rule, only a small number of persons are likely to unite. But the whole description is not that of a sudden isolated outbreak of hostility toward the Christians. There was not only time enough to allow for a change in the mode of prosecution,[7] but the massacre was continued long enough to bring satiety to a populace pretty well accustomed to public butcheries.[8] Suetonius[9] confirms that the persecution lasted for a longer period by enumerating it among a number of permanent police regulations for maintaining order and good conduct. This is quite possible, although Nero, having begun the persecution in 64, left Rome at

---

[1] Seneca—ita incipit.—Ad quae Nero sic ferme respondit. Ann. 14, 53, 55.
[2] 13, 1.   [4] 16, 6.
[3] 14, 2.   [5] 15, 44.
[6] The Church in the Rom. Emp., p. 240.
[7] Igitur primum correpti, qui fatebantur, deinde indicio eorum multitudo ingens haud proinde in crimine incendi quam odio humani generis convicti sunt.
[8] Unde quamquam adversus sontes et novissima exempla meritos miseratio oriebatur, tamquam non utilitate publica, sed in saevitiam unius absumerentur.
[9] Nero, 16.

the end of 66, and only returned in 68 to hear of the revolt of Vinidex: for we know that, going to Greece, he left his hangman Helios at Rome with full power to kill.[1] Origen may seem to contradict Tacitus with regard to the number of Christians killed. In a treatise written in 248 he says: "Only a few, whose numbers can easily be counted, have suffered death from time to time for the sake of the faith, and to encourage the rest."[2] But here is no real disagreement. As Friedlaender points out, the victims of the Neronian persecution, who cannot properly be called martyrs, were not reckoned.[3] The "multitudo ingens" then should seem to offer no difficulty. Besides, why should we assume that the persecutions did not spread beyond the bounds of Rome? True, Tacitus speaks of the City; but he refers to the spreading of Christianity from Judaea to the Capitol. Does he not perhaps after all see the vast multitude scattered over a larger part of the empire? A votive inscription found in the ruins of the village of Marquesia in Lusitania testifies both to the extent and the severity of the persecution.[4] It is not likely that Nero ordered the persecution to be extended to the provinces, except where there was a special occasion for it; but his action at Rome must have served as a precedent in other parts of the empire.

Eusebius of Caesarea confirms the long duration of the Neronian persecution by naming Peter and Paul, the two great apostles of Christ, among the victims.[5] The death of these two apostles occurred, according to Clemens Romanus, in February of the last year of Nero's reign, while he was abroad. The persecution begun in 64 then did not cease before the end of his reign.

It is possible that Nero, although he was absent at the time, was directly responsible for the death of the two apostles, for, departing for the East, the emperor had committed to Helios all whom he had doomed to die.[6]

But what of the charge of "odium humani generis" and the "flagitia" on account of which the Christians were hated? Gibbon[7] says that "it was natural for the philosopher to indulge himself in the description of the origin, the progress, and the character of the new sect, not so much according to the knowledge or prejudices of the age of Nero, as according to those of

[1] Dio C. 63, 12.
[2] Orig. c. Cels. III, 8.
[3] Rom. Life and Manners III, 193.
[4] NERONI. CL. CAIS. AUG. PONT. MAX. OB. PROVINC. LATRONIB. ET. HIS. QUI. NOVAM. GENERI. HUM. SUPERSTITION. INCULCAB. PURGATAM. Inscr. Grut. p. 238, 9. Cp. Paul's Ep. to the Rom. 15, 21.
[5] Eusebius, Hist. eccl., 2, 25.
[6] Dio C. 63, 12.
[7] Rom. Empire I, 604.

the time of Hadrian," and explains the view recorded by Tacitus as due to the fact that he appropriated to the Christians of Rome the guilt and the sufferings which he might have contributed with far greater truth to the followers of Judas the Gaulonite. But this conjecture is, as M. Guizot says, entirely devoid, not merely of verisimilitude, but even of possibility, because the followers of Judas never went to Rome and can hardly have been known as a sect, and because Tacitus refers too distinctly to the etymology of the name of Christians to allow us to suspect any mistake on his part.[1]

As to the *"hatred of mankind,"* the MS. of Florence has "coniuncti" instead of "convicti." Ramsay,[2] who adopts this reading, considers it a poetical usage in the sense: They were put side by side with the first class of culprits.[3] But not only must we suspect that "coniuncti" is the correction of a Christian copyist, but the verb of the first clause, "correpti," seems to require the corresponding "convicti sunt," since the intent evidently is not to record the opinion of the public, nor even of the courts, but the prosecution of the Christians. Tacitus no doubt meant to say that the Christians were convicted of the crime of "odium."

By the *"flagitia"* probably poisoning and magic were meant. Tacitus does not say that the Christians were believed to commit such crimes,[4] but that they were hated on account of them. The words contain a judgment of the writer upon the Christians that we can not get away from.

It is not at all incredible, however, that such crimes were attributed to the private meetings of the Christians from the beginning,[5] as we know they were later on. Friedlaender has remarked that in the old Roman world the impression caused by the great Bacchanalia process (185 B. C.) lasted for centuries. "At that time," he says, "a secret worship of Bacchus that had made its way into Rome through Etruria was used as a cloak for the most outrageous excesses and the most abominable crimes; the result of the investigation instituted by the senate was the punishment (chiefly by death) of thousands who had taken part in these orgies. The charges of Oedipean connections and Thyestean banquets (i. e. unnatural excesses and ritual murder) were revived against the Christians."[6] The error of Tacitus then is reduced to this that he records as facts the "flagitia," of which the Christians were falsely accused. It

[1] Gibbon, Rom. Empire 1, 605, note.
[2] The Church in the Rom. Emp. p. 233, note.
[3] Cp. Ann. 13, 7; 6, 26; 4, 57, 33.
[4] This is Ramsay's interpretation, p. 237.
[5] Cp. 1. Peter 2, 12: "They speak against you as evildoers."
[6] L. Friedlaender, Rom. Life and Manners III, 189.

would not be fair to make any inference from this instance with regard to the character of his research generally. The error can be explained, partly by the obscurity of the Christians in those days, whom Tacitus considered a Jewish sect,[1] partly by the pride of the old Roman, who hardly could deem such a foreign matter, which seemed of so little consequence to the state, worthy of any investigation beyond that of the courts. Judgments like that of Pliny[2] were no doubt rare exceptions, and even Pliny would perhaps not have arrived at his more correct view of Christianity, if it had not been his official duty to inquire into the matter.

Chronology

Employing the annalistic method, Tacitus gives the chronological sequence of events with much accuracy. When relating the history of wars or of foreign affairs, he sometimes brings together events of more than one year; but in these instances he does not fail to state it,[3] or the chronology is apparent without any explanation.[4]

Superstition

Like other writers of his time, Tacitus was *not free from superstition*. In the career of Curtius Rufus, the son of a gladiator who finally obtained the consular power, the honors of triumph and the government of Africa, he saw the fulfillment of a prediction by a vision.[5] He records as a fact that the Ubians in 58 A. D. were afflicted by mysterious fire, issuing from the earth, which could be put out only by volleys of stones and blows from clubs, and by the throwing on of clothes, which proved the more effectual, the more soiled and worn they were.[6] The appearance of a comet in 60 A. D. is recorded as presaging a change of rulers.[7] Nero's bathing in the sacred water of the fountainhead of the Marcian aqueduct brought upon him a dangerous sickness showing the wrath of the gods.[8] The superstition of Tacitus does not, however, materially affect the value of his work, as he is moderate in recording such things. In fact, it must be borne in mind that, though the historian himself should be free from superstition, any history of a superstitious people would be imperfect without a record of such things be-

[1] Cp. G. Boissier, Tacite. p. 148-49.
[2] Ep. ad Traj. 96.
[3] Ann. 13, 9.
[4] 14, 23. cp. with 13, 41., the respective years being 58 and 60.
[5] 11, 21.
[6] 13, 57.
[7] 14, 22.
[8] 14, 22.

cause of their influence upon the affairs of the state and of individuals.[1]

Suggestion of Motives

The fondness of Tacitus for suggesting motives is remarkable and has been criticised. It should be noted, however, that he is very *careful in determining the motives* in any case. As a rule, he mentions a number of possible or probable motives, leaving it to the judgment of the reader to decide which was the real motive;[2] and in this respect he differs from Suetonius and Dio Cassius. However difficult the task may be, it can not be considered a fault, if the historian tries to bring out the psychological element of history.

Preponderance of the Personal Element

In this connection we may consider that the personality of Nero occupies so large a place in the story of his reign, that, in spite of the annalistic form of the work, it is, in substance, *almost biographical*. The historical works of the imperial period are all, more or less, characterized by a concentration upon the mere personal element.[3] In the history of Nero this is not a serious fault, if a fault at all. Tacitus always has in view the influence of Nero's acts upon the whole Roman state. Clason has well said: "Wenn er auch keine Biographie des Kaisers schrieb, so blieb doch die Person desselben durchaus das bewegende Moment in der Zeit, daher denn sein Charakter vor Allem zur noetigen Klarheit und Durchsichtigkeit gebracht werden musste. Wie weit dies Tacitus gelungen ist, und ob bei Nero es ueberhaupt moeglich war, ist eine andere Frage. Eine aehnliche Mischung des uebermuetigen, eitlen, leichtfertigen, furchtsamen und unbesonnenen Kindes mit dem vor keinem Verbrechen zurueckschreckenden, gewissenlosesten und sittlich verwahrlosesten, dabei mit Talenten begabten Manne, ist kaum jemals vorhanden gewesen, eine Mischung, bei der das Verstaendnis aufhoert und des Historikers groesste Kunst darin besteht, das Ungeheuerliche in seiner Vereinigung zu einer Person recht anschaulich darzustellen."[4]

---

[1] Cp. Ann. 13, 57: the superstition of the Hermundurians and the Chattians as a cause of the battle; 13, 58: the effect of the withering of the tree Ruminalis upon the mind of the people; 13, 13: the storms and pestilences by which the gods branded the year that was stained with so much blood prepared the mind of the people for the overthrow of Nero; 15, 47: vulgantur prodigia, imminentium malorum nuntia.
[2] Cp. Ann. 13, 18; 14, 59; 15, 38.
[3] Teuffel and Schwabe, History of Rom. Lit. 1, 54.
[4] Clason, Tac. p. Suet., p. 16.

Characterization of Nero

Among the stronger traits of Nero's character, Tacitus emphasizes his *cruelty*. Did he consider this trait the dominating one? Perhaps not; but it is Nero's influence upon the state that interests Tacitus most; and to the state the emperor's cruelty proved more destructive than his vanity and sensuality. Tacitus is therefore sometimes misled to disregard the chief motive of an action or to treat it as secondary. Relating the death of C. Petronius, Tacitus says: "Tigellinus had recourse to the cruelty of the prince, a passion to which all his other passions gave place, laying to the charge of Petronius an intimacy with Scaevinus."[1] In this case the cruelty was evidently aroused by fear; for Scaevinus had been chosen to fell Nero in the conspiracy of Piso. In fact most of the innumerable acts of cruelty that Nero committed were prompted either by fear or by a desire to possess the wealth of his victims for the purpose of satisfying his vanity and sensuality. It would be difficult to find an instance in which the emperor perpetrated a cruelty merely because he took pleasure in inflicting suffering upon others. Most of his cruel acts were due to other traits of his character.[2] These Tacitus does not overlook. He says e. g. of the young prince that his vices, as yet undeveloped, agreed remarkably with the avarice and prodigality of Narcissus.[3] He mentions that Nero destroyed Pallas, because the protracted life of the freedman kept him out of the riches this man had accumulated,[4] and that to the rapacity of the prince multitudes owed their destruction.[5] He records how those who were doomed by the emperor to die remembered him in their wills, in order that he might spare their relatives.[6] He furthermore describes how Nero was overpowered with terror and dismay, when he heard that his plan to destroy his mother had failed and could not be unknown to her;[7] and once he makes the statement that Nero was always timorous.[8] He also furnishes many proofs of the extreme vanity of Nero, who "longed to achieve things that exceeded credibility,"[9] and opposed, banished, or killed men, because they possessed greater talent than he, or failed to recognize his pretended superiority.[10] All this is not lacking in Tacitus:[11] but in his plan

---

[1] Ann. 16, 18. Cp. 15, 58: magis magisve pavido Nerone.
[2] Cp. Dio C. 61, 5. We can apply to Nero Suetonius' judgment on Domitian: super ingenii naturam inopia rapax, metu saevus, Suet. Dom. 3.
[3] Ann. 13, 1.
[4] 14, 65.
[5] 16, 14.
[6] 16, 11. 17.
[7] 14, 7.
[8] 16, 5.
[9] 15, 42.
[10] 15, 49 (Lucan); 16, 29 (Montanus); 16, 21 (Thrasea Paetus).
[11] Cp. also 14, 13: superbus ac publici servitii victor.

of presentation the destructive cruelty of Nero demands emphasis, and therefore the other traits of the emperor's character are not brought out as strongly as they should be and in their proper relation to his cruelty and to each other.

SUETONIUS

Character

Suetonius is described by the younger Pliny, who was his intimate friend, as a studious man, who was not easily moved to publish the fruit of his studies.[1] That Pliny assisted him in providing for the publication of his works, seems to indicate that Suetonius was a man of retired habits, unfamiliar with practical affairs of life.[2] Pliny entertained the highest regard for him and valued his impartial judgment. In his letter to Trajan, in which he asks the emperor to grant to his friend the "ius trium liberorum," he calls him: "probissimum honestissimum eruditissimum virum."[3] But learned, truth-loving, and diligent though he was, Suetonius was hardly familiar enough with the affairs of the world and the life of the empire to write a work that would give us a true picture of Nero and his time.

Scope and Plan of His Life of Nero

A history of the empire under Nero's reign he did not, however, aim at giving us. While Tacitus presents Nero as the head of the state and describes him as seen in his relation to the events of that time, Suetonius describes the personality of Nero taken for itself, paying no regard to the general course of the history of the empire. His life of Nero is not even a real history of the emperor's life, but only a mass of biographical material arranged in a number of groups.

Ausonius divides his Life into four sections: name, exploits, manner of life, death.[4] The arrangement of the material might be indicated in the following way. After recording Nero's pedigree, his birth, and early youth up to the time of his accession, he illustrates in succession various traits of the emperor's character in the following order. Chapter 10: Clemency and justice in the early part of his reign; 11-13: fondness for games and exhibitions; 14-17: attention to the affairs of the state; 18: ambition for the extension of the empire; 19: journies abroad;

[1] Plin. ep. 1, 24; 5, 10.
[2] Peter, Die gesch. Lit., 2, 67: ein aengstlicher Stubengelehrter.
[3] Ad Traj., 94, 1.
[4] De XII Caes. 1, 4-5: Nomina res gestas vitamque obitumque peregit.

20-25: disgraceful passions; 26-39: criminal qualities (petulantia, libido, luxuria, avaritia, crudelitas); 40-45: his downfall; 51: his physical person; 52: literary activity; 53-55: vanity; 56: irreligiousness; 57: death.

Value of the Work

The plan did not permit of much chronology nor of much consideration of cause and effect. Consequently the picture which Suetonius draws, if it may be called a picture, lacks a background. Besides, the different parts are out of proportion with each other. There are e. g. nine chapters on Nero's theatre-craze,[1] while there are only six on his cruelties,[2] although the latter are historically more important. Clason's description of the biography is true: "Fuer Sueton ist alles ein plattes Bild, auf dem die Momente neben einander, teils groesser, teils kleiner stehen, in dem keine Perspektive, keine Ursache fuer Klein und Gross, Hell and Dunkel existiert. Ein solches Bild hat keinen Charakter und ist qualitativ wertlos."[3] Take e. g. the persecution of the Christians. While Tacitus tells us that it was resorted to by Nero after the conflagration to avert from himself the hatred of the suffering people,[4] Suetonius simply mentions it as a police regulation among the laudable acts of Nero.[5]

The value of the work lies chiefly in its many biographical and other details, by which the narrative of Tacitus is illustrated or supplemented, and sometimes corrected. It supplies information, e. g., on public opinion concerning the punishment of the Christians in 64 A. D., the occasion of Nero's tour to Greece and his participation in the contests, the Golden House before and after the great fire, the attempted digging of the Campanian canal, the influence a comet had on the prosecution of the Pisonian conspirators, and the details of Nero's plan of revenge near the end and his subsequent plans of escape.[6]

Relation to Tacitus

Suetonius never names Tacitus. As the intimate friend of the younger Pliny he must, however, have known Tacitus and his works. Tacitus was no doubt among their common friends to whom Pliny had announced the publication of Suetonius' works.[7]

[1] Suet. Nero 11-13; 20-25.
[2] 33-38.
[3] Clason, Tac. u. Suet. p. 20.
[4] Ann. 15, 44.
[5] Nero 16.
[6] Nero 16 (multa animadversa severe et coercita—afflicti supplicils Christiani); 22-24; 31; 31-32; 36; 43; 47.
[7] Plin. ep. 5, 10.

The question then arises: Did Suetonius use the Annals of Tacitus in writing his Life of Nero, and to what extent?

The two authors differ not only by each recording facts which the other does not mention,[1] which might be due to a difference of plan, but also on events which both record.

The former is the case with regard to the construction of the great wooden theatre on the Campus Martius. Suetonius,[2] to show Nero's fondness for games and exhibitions, records both the construction of the theatre and the spectacles given at its dedication. Tacitus[3] turns from the subject with disgust, remarking that it is unworthy of being inserted in the annals of the Roman people.

For the latter a considerable number of examples could be adduced. According to Suetonius[4] Nero was born on the 15th day of December in the year 37 A. D. and was adopted by Claudius in the boy's 11th year, in the year 48 or 49.[5] According to Tacitus[6] the adoption did not take place before the beginning of the year 50, when Nero was in his 13th year. Tacitus is evidently right, as he names the consuls of the year, and Claudius did not marry Agrippina before the year 49.[7] While Tacitus attributes the attempt at incest to Agrippina,[8] Suetonius says that it was Nero's desire to enter into an incestuous relation to his mother, and claims that this had not been considered a matter of doubt by any one.[9] There is also a noteworthy difference concerning the poetical productions of the emperor. Tacitus,[10] as we have seen, claims that Nero's poems were largely the productions of others, and bases this judgment on the alleged lack of uniformity. Suetonius[11] says the opposite, that Nero composed poems with pleasure and ease. He claims to have seen Nero's manuscripts and to have observed that the poems bore the marks of being one man's work. The divergence could not be greater. Besides, Suetonius remarks that some believed that Nero had published the works of others under his own name.[12] Was Tacitus among the authors he refers to? If not, his sources must have been. Again, while Tacitus calls it a rumor that Nero during the conflagration of Rome sang the

---

[1] Cp. the abolition of the decrees of Claudius. Suet. Nero 34, which Tacitus does not record.
[2] Nero 12.
[3] Ann. 13, 31.
[4] Nero 6-7.
[5] Nero 7 compared with 6: "post VIIII. mensem quam Tiberius, excessit," and Tiberius 73: "anno tertio et vicesimo imperii. XVII. KAL. Ap.
[6] Ann. 12, 25.
[7] Suet. Claud. 26; Joseph. Ant. 20, 8, 1; Tac. Ann. 12, 5: C. Pompeio Q. Verannio consulibus. Cp. Dio C. 60, 31.
[8] Ann. 14, 2.
[9] Nero 28.
[10] 14, 16.
[11] Nero 52.
[12] ut quidam putant.

Destruction of Troy, Suetonius states it as a fact; and while according to Tacitus Nero was said to have done this on the stage of the imperial theatre,[1] Suetonius names the Tower of Maecenas as the place.[2]

These examlpes show that Suetonius wrote his biography quite independently of the Annals of Tacitus,[3] and that he must have had some sources that Tacitus did not possess; for if he had no other sources, Tacitus would have had to record these divergencies in accordance with his rule.[4] Above we have mentioned Suetonius' reference to manuscripts of Nero that he had studied.[5] This reference indicates the sources that were at his disposal, but not at the disposal of Tacitus; they were in the imperial archives, which his position as private secretary to Hadrian gave him access to. Perhaps he was also more inclined to listen to verbal tradition,[6] as he did not hesitate to record the vilest lampoons.[7] At any rate, he used original sources, though, on the whole, they must have been the same that Tacitus used. Besides, the time of the composition of the two works makes it almost certain that Suetonius did not use Tacitus. The Annals appeared only a short time before the publication of Suetonius' Lives, and Suetonius' mode of composition presupposes a longer time.[8]

Use of Sources

In the use of his sources, Suetonius is not guided by the principle that we have seen Tacitus follow. While Tacitus e. g. states that Nero killed Poppaea by a kick, but also mentions the report that she was poisoned,[9] Suetonius gives us the former version only.[10] While Tacitus records that it is uncertain whether Burrus was poisoned by Nero or died of a throat disease,[11] Suetonius makes the positive statement that Burrus died of poison administered by the order of Nero.[12] Concerning the cause of the great fire, Tacitus again mentions two reports, the one affirming that it was accidental, the other that Nero had set the City afire;[13] Suetonius simply says that Nero caused the fire.[14] According to Tacitus, there was a false report among the

[1] Ann. 15, 39.
[2] Nero 38.
[3] Clason, Suet. u. Tac., p. 27.
[4] Ann. 13, 20.
[5] Nero 52. Cp. Aug. 87.
[6] Nero 29: ex nonnullis comperi. Cp. Claud. 15: a majoribus natu audiebam.
[7] Nero 39.
[8] Peter, Die geschichtl. Lit. 2, 69.
[9] Ann. 16, 6.
[10] Nero 35.
[11] Ann. 11, 51.
[12] Nero 35.
[13] Ann. 15, 38.
[14] Nero 29.

Syrian troops during the Armenian war, spread by the Parthians, that Roman legions under Paetus had been made to pass under the yoke.[1] Suetonius states this humiliation as an established fact.[2]

These examples do not prove that Suetonius generally followed one author as his main source and only in rare cases consulted several;[3] but they show that, as a rule, he does not record any divergence of his sources. This is a fault which appears the more serious, as we notice what determined his choice in such cases. As suggested by the plan of his work, it was his interest to illustrate certain traits of character in the emperor. Take e. g. the great fire.[4] If Suetonius wanted to record it at all, he had to group it, according to his plan, with some other events illustrating the same trait of Nero's character. That Nero was suspected and by many believed to have set fire to the City, was a fact that all were agreed on. But Suetonius makes the positive statement: "incendit urbem." The proofs, however, which he adduces are not at all convincing. That Nero once uttered the wish to outlive, like Priam, the destruction of his mother-city— and Suetonius does not even put it as directly as that—is no proof that he set fire to Rome, and that at this time, when he still believed his reign secure; that some of Nero's servants were discovered with tow and torch on the property of others, might be explained by the fact that attempts were made to save in this way those parts of the City which adjoined the burning sections; this is also the simplest explanation for the destruction of the granaries near the Golden House by the use of machines of war and by fire; Tacitus records that in this way the fire was actually stopped on the sixth day;[5] and was not the vanity of Nero great enough to permit him to attempt a theatrical stunt in the midst of a calamity which he himself had good reason to deplore? But Nero setting fire to his imperial city—what a splendid illustration of his insane cruelty, which did not let him spare even "his people and the walls of the city of his fathers."[6] From Tacitus we learn that there was no evidence of Nero's guilt.[7]

Using his sources in this way, Suetonius could not, of course, be consistent in his choice between divergent records. Take the death of Nero. In his biography of the Emperor he tells us that Epaphroditus a libellis aided his master in killing himself; in the life of Domitian, who condemned Epaphroditus to death, he will

[1] Ann. 15, 15.
[2] Nero 39.
[3] Nero 34: viewing of the mother's body.
[4] Nero 38.
[5] Ann. 15, 40.
[6] Nero 38.
[7] Ann. 15, 38.

not say more than that this officer was believed to have lent a hand when Nero put an end to his life.[1]

Neither can the research of Suetonius have been very exhaustive. He was not always aware of the existence of divergent reports which others have recorded. The question of Nero's incest is such a case. We know from Tacitus[2] that there was a difference of opinion between the older historians as to whether the incestuous approaches proceeded from Nero or from Agrippina. Nevertheless Suetonius tells us: "That Nero sought sexual intercourse with his mother * * * no one has doubted.[3]

On the other hand, there is a peculiar definiteness in Suetonius. Take his statements of time and place. Nero was born at Antium "post VIII mensem quam Tiberius excessit, XVIII KL. JAN. tantum quod exoriente sole, paene ut radiis prius quam terra contingeretur."[4] The marriage of Poppaea Sabina took place "duodecimo die post divortium Octaviae."[5] He states the exact duration of each of the four consulates of Nero.[6] The place of the fallen emperor's last refuge is described as "inter Salariam et Nomentanam viam circa quartam miliarium."[7] May we then not assume that as far as his method permitted him, and the extent of his research enabled him to be, Suetonius was as accurate in his statements as he was definite?

Statement of Motives

Suetonius rarely suggests or attempts to determine motives, but lets the items he records speak for themselves. He is an antiquarian, not a philosopher.

Influence of Antiquarian Interest

His antiquarian interest is in evidence throughout the Life of Nero. Brief as he otherwise is, he deems the story of the origin of the name Aenobarbus worthy of record.[8] As to the great fire, he deplores most the loss of the many monuments of antiquity,[9] and uses more words in stating these than other losses that were really greater. He explains why Nero on his tour in Greece did not dare to seek initiation into the Eleusinian mysteries.[10] He notices that when the report of the desertion of the armies reached the emperor while at breakfast, he dashed against the

[1] Nero 49; Dom. 11.
[2] Ann. 14, 2.
[3] Nero 28.
[4] Nero 6.
[5] Nero 35.
[6] Nero 14.
[7] Nero 48.
[8] Nero 1.
[9] Nero 38: quidquid visendum atque memorabile ex antiquitate duraverat.
[10] Nero 34.

floor two of his favorite cups, on which Homeric scenes were embossed.[1] And he records that Nero in his last hours desired to hear an explanation of the punishment "more maiorum."[2]

To the historian such things are of minor value. Sometimes, it is true, they cast light upon the character of Nero, and it must be remembered that this was the aim of Suetonius.[3] Frequently however they take the place of more important information. The extent of the influence of this antiquarian interest upon his mode of presentation or the choice of material may be seen from the last example. Nero had in his hiding place received a letter to the effect that the senate had declared him an enemy of the fatherland and was seeking him, in order that he might be punished "more maiorum." He then asked, says Suetonius, what sort of punishment that was. Could Nero really be ignorant on this point? He had studied and written history. He knew of the institution of his ancestors "to withdraw from sight the bodies of such as died prematurely."[4] We are inclined to think that Suetonius let Nero inquire as to the mode of punishment, in order to gain an opportunity to answer the question himself.

Partiality for Gossip and Discreditable Facts

The antiquarian interest of Suetonius is coupled with a strong partiality for discreditable things. Gossip and scandal have found too much credence with him and too large a place in his work.[5] We need but refer to his minute and comprehensive records of Nero's sexual outrages.[6]

Characterization of Nero

Suetonius' characterization of Nero differs somewhat from that of the Annals. Describing the evil traits of the emperor's character,[7] he speaks of his recklessness, licentiousness, avarice, and cruelty. Which of these he considers the strongest is not clear. There is nothing to indicate any comparison. His cruelty is at least not emphasized, as in Tacitus. It is worth noting, however, that Nero's vanity, not mentioned here, is treated by itself in three of the concluding chapters,[8] and that his theatrical activities, in which his vanity found the most pronounced ex-

---
[1] Nero 47.
[2] Nero 49.
[3] Compare Nero 2: Pluris e familia cognosci referre arbitror, quo facilius appareat ita degenerasse e suorum virtutibus Nero, ut tamen vitia cuiusque quasi tradita et ingenita retulerit.
[4] Tac. Ann. 13, 17. A motion that Antistius should be killed more maiorum had been reported to him by the consuls of A. D. 62. Tac. Ann. 14, 49. He had interposed when the punishment "more maiorum" was recommended in another case. 16, 11.
[5] Sandys, Comp. to Lat. Stud., p. 1011.
[6] Nero 28-29.
[7] Nero 26-39.
[8] 53-55.

pression, are described in no less than nine chapters,¹ while only six are given to the relation of his cruelties.²

The licentiousness of the emperor too, though not expressly emphasized, stands out more glaring than in the Annals. This is partly explained, but only partly, by Clason's remark on Tacitus: "Der Gegenstand war zu ekelhaft, um detailliert zu werden."³ Tacitus could not, of course, have embodied chapters 28-29 of Suetonius' Life in his Annals, while on the other hand, as we have seen, Suetonius is fond of recording gossip and scandal. But it would be unfair to assume that Suetonius was here led only by his fondness for the scandalous, and had no serious purpose. All the horrible details lead up to a statement of Nero's moral principle: "neminem hominem pudicum aut ulla corporis parte purum esse, verum plerosque dissimulare vitium et callide optegere."⁴ He considers the emperor's licentiousness a "naturae vitium, non aetatis."⁵ To establish this claim is one of the objects Suetonius has in view, when describing the ancestors of Nero. While the emperor's grandfather, who by his marriage with Antonia, the Elder, the niece of Augustus, established the connection of his family with the Julian house, was a man of vice, Nero's father, Cn. Domitius Aenobarbus, was "omni parte vitae detestabilis," and among his crimes Suetonius makes special mention of incest with his sister Lepida.⁶ These two among Nero's ancestors, at least, seem to have been described with a view to inherited traits in the emperor.

We may then conclude from the record of Suetonius that vanity and sensuality were the dominating traits in the character of Nero. They were combined with great recklessness, bordering at times on insanity, but quickly giving way to fright and dismay, and they led to extravagance, avarice, and cruelty, without which his vanity and sensuality could not be satisfied.

DIO CASSIUS

Valuation

That the Roman History of Dio Cassius, published in the beginning of the third century, was not considered unimportant is seen from the large number of fragments preserved in various writers, from the continuation of his work by an unknown to the

¹11-13, 20-25.
²33-38.
³Clason, Tac. und Suet., p. 20.
⁴Nero 29.
⁵Nero 26.
⁶Nero 1 and 5.

time of Constantine, and from the abridgment of Xiphilinus and the numerous excerpts from it in the Annals of Zonaras.

Modern historiography has relegated Dio to a much inferior position. Sihler considers him incredibly reckless and finds his ignorance sometimes painful, his reasoning weak, his allusions often pointless, and some of the material of his work too poor to notice in detail;[1] and Henderson thinks he is "little better than a second-hand Suetonius writing in a pseudo-Thucydidean style."[2]

Opportunity for Research

It must be conceded, however, that Dio had ample opportunity for research. He was senator under Commodus, governor of Smyrna after the death of Septimius Severus (211 A. D.), afterward consul, as also proconsul in Africa and Panonia. Alexander Severus (222-235) made him consul for the second time. He not only spent the greater part of his time in public employments that afforded opportunity for historical studies, but his relation to Alexander Severus must have given him access to valuable historical documents not accessible to others. Likely his claim that he had read nearly everything that had been written by anybody on the events recorded in his history[3] was justified.

Veracity

The fact that Alexander Severus, whose character was highly praiseworthy, entertained such high regard for him that he made him consul for the second time, with himself, although the praetorian guard, irritated against Dio on account of his severity, had demanded his life, leads us to assume that he was a truth-loving man, and endeavored both to find and to present the truth.

It must not be forgotten, however, that Dio had to spend eighteen years of his life under the reign of a cruel tyrant, and that the life and reign of Septimius Severus presented many points of striking similarity to that of Nro. Moreover, Dio was in disfavor with that emperor and held no office during his reign. It would therefore not have been inconsistent with the veracity with which he is credited, if, when writing the history of Nero, he had been inclined to overdraw, just as Tacitus had been.

Sources

Dio seldom makes definite mention of sources, and never in the history of Nero, as far as can be seen from the abridgment.

[1] Cic. of Arpin., p. 169, 437.
[2] The Life and Princ. of the E. N. Prol., p. 11.
[3] Dio C. 1, 2.

Once he mentions Decianus Catus, the governor of Britain, as his authority for the cause of the British revolt;[1] but he does not state where he found a record of the testimony. "As they say," "it is said," "I have heard," "as has been said by many trustworthy men,"[2] and similar phrases constitute his references; but this he has in common with all the ancient historians. These references, however indefinite, when compared with such declarations of Dio as the one in 53, 19, 6,[3] sufficiently warrant the assumption that he used all the sources that were at his disposal, and, as seen, they can not have been so very few.

Method

How he used them, is a question of greater importance. He describes his method in 53, 19, 6.[3] The passage occurs in the history of Augustus, but is so general that it may be taken to apply to other parts of his work as well.

In the first place, then, it is a principle with Dio to tell us what has been officially recorded on the affairs of the empire, whether the official records contain the truth or not. But he will not do so uncritically. Where it is necessary, he will correct the official version in accordance with what he has read or heard or seen. Applied to the history of Nero and his reign, this would mean that with the documents in the imperial archives and the records of the Journals of the City, Dio has compared the testimony of preceding historians, verbal tradition, and historical monuments.

Relation to Tacitus and Suetonius

If Dio has really followed this method, the passage disproves the one-source theory, according to which Dio's work, as far as the history of Nero is concerned, shall have consisted chiefly in transcribing the Annals of Tacitus.

No extensive comparison of Dio's history with the Annals is necessary to show that the theory is actually ill supported. Compare, e. g. the reports of the two authors on *the destruction of Agrippina*.[4] Tacitus says that Anicetus, the commander of the fleet at Misenum, who was hated by and hated Agrippina, devised the plan to kill her and offered it to Nero while the em-

---

[1] 62, 2.
[2] 58, 23; 58, 23; 58, 11; 61, 21.
[3] ὅθενπερ καὶ ἐγὼ πάντα τὰ ἑξῆς, ὅσα γε καὶ ἀναγκαῖον ἔσται εἰπεῖν, ὡς που καὶ δεδήλωται φράσω, εἴτ' ὄντως οὕτως εἴτε καὶ ἑτέρως πως ἔχει. προσέσται μέντοι τι αὐτοῖς καὶ τῆς ἐμῆς δοξασίας, ἐς ὅσον ἐνδέχεται, ἐν οἷς ἄλλο τι μᾶλλον ἢ τὸ θρυλούμενον ἠδυνήθην ἐκ πολλῶν ὧν ἀνέγνων ἢ καὶ ἤκουσα ἢ καὶ εἶδον τεκμήρασθαι.
[4] Tac. Ann. 14, 3. seq.; Dio C. 61, 12. seq.

peror was at Baiae, keeping the holidays of the Quinquatrus, and he says expressly that it is not clear whether Seneca and Burrus knew of the plan, before it was executed. According to Dio the plan was suggested to Seneca and Nero when one day in the theatre they saw a ship falling to pieces, emitting wild animals, and that Nero thereafter went to Campania to execute it.

According to Tacitus Agrippina traveled to Antium in a litter, was there met by Nero and conducted to Bauli. Dio says that having gone to Campania and having received his mother (in Campania, of course), Nero sailed with her to Bauli on the navis dolosa.

Tacitus then mentions that the plan of Nero was betrayed to Agrippina, and that instead of using the ship which Nero had presented to her at Bauli, she traveled to Baiae in a litter, that her fears however were overcome at Baiae by the dissimulation of Nero, and that here she was induced to board the ship. Dio has nothing of all this, but records gorgeous banquets at Bauli and Agrippina's sailing from this port.

According to Tacitus the mechanism of the ship could not be made to function properly, so that the ship did not fall to pieces, but, the upper part of the ship being wrecked, a falling ceiling killed Crepereius Gallus, one of Agrippina's two attendants. Dio here contradicts Tacitus, saying that the ship did fall apart.

By Tacitus we are told that, as the mechanism did not function properly, the crew bore the vessel down on one side in order to sink it, and that in this way Argippina and her maid were thrown into the sea, while Dio sees her falling into the sea, as the ship falls apart.

Surely, these differences can not be explained by mere negligence on the part of the supposed transcriber of the Annals.

Or take Dio's record of *Nero's encounter with Julius Montanus* during one of the emperor's nightly escapades in 56 A. D. Tacitus, we notice, only says that Montanus, having encountered the emperor, vehemently repelled him.[1] But Dio states that Nero assaulted the wife of Montanus, and that Montanus then gave Nero such a handling that the emperor had to keep indoors for several days with black eyes.[2] There is another difference here. While both state that Montanus, recognizing Nero after the conflict, apologized, and for this reason was put to death, Tacitus relates the event to show why Nero thereafter became more careful and used the services of soldiers and gladiators

[1] Ann. 13, 25.
[2] Dio C. 61, 9.

when on these nightly tours, and, of course, with the further object of showing to what extent Nero indulged this craze, Dio uses the incident to show that Nero was not revengeful, as Montanus would not have been killed, if he had not shown that he had recognized the emperor.

Dio has a definite *charge of usury against Seneca*. He tells us that the philosopher had compelled the Britons to accept immense sums at interest for the purpose of meeting obligations resulting from the tyranny of Claudius, and by his unrelenting demands of payment caused the insurrection.[1] Tacitus has only a reference to a general charge of usury against Seneca in the self-defense of Suilius,[2] which occurred in the year 58, while the British revolt took place in 61.

While Tacitus states that the cause of the death of Burrus is uncertain,[3] Dio says that Nero removed Burrus by means of poison.[4]

These and other examples show that Dio did not merely transcribe from Tacitus, however much he may have used his work. That certain passages seem to have been translated from Tacitus, is no proof to the contrary; for in other parts of Dio's history, where transcription is out of the question, we find other authors occasionally utilized in the same way.[5] He may have used Tacitus for his history of Nero, as he used Livy for other parts of his work, omitting and protracting according to his taste or interest.[6] But such use would not preclude that he also used other sources as much as they merited.[7]

Dio offers some information that we can get from no other source. He tells us of the effect of the prince's inaugural speech in the Praetorian camp and in the senate. Although it was known to have been written by Seneca, it helped very much to secure the government to Nero. The senate passed a resolution to have the document read whenever the consuls would enter upon their office, and had it engraved upon a silver tablet for a public record.[8] Concerning the relation of the freedman Pallas to Agrippina and to the government in the beginning of Nero's reign, Dio records that Pallas even appeared in public with the emperor's mother, lying in the same lectica, and that Pallas received embassies and wrote letters to peoples and rulers.[9] From

[1] Dio C. 61, 1-2.
[2] Ann. 13, 43.
[3] Ann. 14, 51.
[4] Dio C. 62, 13.
[5] Cp. Dio C. 46, 8, with Cic. Phil. 61: Quam miserum est, id negare non posse, quod sit turpissimum confiteri. (Sihler, Cic. of Arp., p. 438.)
[6] Sihler, Cic. of Arp., p. 169.
[7] Pauly-Wissowa, Realenc. d. klass. Altert., III, 1714: Die Frage, ob Tacitus direkt benutzt ist, duerfte heutzutage wohl einstimmig von den Urteilsfaehigen verneint werden.—Schwartz.
[8] Dio C. 61, 3.
[9] 61, 3.

Dio we learn that Seneca and Burrus, who, after the incident at the reception of the Armenian embassy in 54 A. D.,[1] had controlled the affairs of the government, no longer had such a hold on Nero after the death of Britannicus.[2] It is Dio who tells us of the accusations brought against Seneca in 57 A. D., among which were those of adultery, pederasty, and extravagance, the two last of which charges he holds to have been true.[3] Regarding the divorce of Octavia, Dio informs us that Burrus took the part of Octavia,[4] which seems to explain the circumstance related by Tacitus that when, soon after the death of Burrus, Octavia was, divorced by Nero, the house of Burrus was assigned to her,[5] and indicates that not only the common people, but also the soldiers of the guard sympathized with her. Seneca, we are told, before his death entrusted his writings to the care of some friends, fearing that Nero might destroy them.[6] Dio also tells us that Nero planned to write a history of Rome in hexameters, on which occasion Annaeus Cornutus played the dangerous role of literary advisor to the emperor, escaping with banishment as a punishment for disagreeable advice.[7] Dio alone records that during Nero's tour in Greece a freedman by the name of Helios had unlimited power in Rome, power to confiscate, banish, and kill plebeians, knights, and senators without conferring with Nero, so that the Roman state at that time was actually serving two emperors.[8] This, of course, tended to hasten the downfall of Nero.[9] When the body-guard deserted the emperor, they were obeying an order of the senate.[10] When the horsemen in search of the condemned emperor approached his hiding place, Nero commanded those who were with him to kill both him and themselves, and being much wrought up when they did not obey, he attempted in vain to kill Sporos.[11] Finally, Dio's record of the events of the last two years of Nero's reign and of his death, being so much more detailed than that of Suetonius, has become our main source for this period through the circumstance that the corresponding part of the Annals of Tacitus has been lost.

As to Suetonius, the difference with regard to the plan of the two authors and the scope of their works is so great as to preclude any extensive use of Suetonius by Dio.

[1] 61. 3.
[2] 61. 7.
[3] 61. 10.
[4] 62. 13.
[5] Ann. 14, 51. 60.
[6] Dio C. 62, 25.
[7] 62, 29.
[8] 63, 12.
[9] Cp. Dio C. 63, 19: Helios urging Nero to return to Rome, because a great conspiracy was forming. (Suet. Nero 23.)
[10] Dio C. 63, 27; Zonaras 11, 13.
[11] Dio C. 63, 29; Zonaras 11, 13.

Faults of Dio's Historiography

Dio's history of Nero is, however, faulty in more than one respect.

In the first place, we notice in Dio a strong desire to entertain, which evidently misleads him to sacrifice historical truth to dramatic effect.

It is interesting to notice that in the only part of the history of Nero for which Dio mentions a definite source,[1] he portrays the British amazon Bundovica, displaying even the length of her golden hair.[2] Much of this may have been taken from memoirs of Suetonius Paulinus; such, we know, he wrote on his expedition to the Atlas in 41 A. D.[3] Nevertheless, this is Dio's manner. The whole description is too detailed to be true. Then take Dio's description of the great conflagration; it is a piece of brilliant narrative, but not an historical record of events.[4] Or compare his description of the beauty and luxury of Poppaea,[5] or that of the coronation of Tiridates at Rome,[6] to which he devotes so much space, or of Nero's triumphal entry into Rome after his athletic and theatrical victories in Greece.[7] Thucydides says: "The absence of romance in my history will perhaps lose it the popular ear. But it will be enough if it is judged useful by those who may desire an accurate knowledge."[8] Dio could not have prefaced his history with such a remark.

In some of the *speeches* we find in Dio, he imitates, like other historians, a characteristic of the work of Thucydides, but he does so in a poor way, a pseudo-Thucydidean way, as Henderson calls it. Here too his desire to be entertaining is too great; it results in gross exaggerations. Take, e. g. the speech of Bundovica,[9] which is an oration on Roman extortion and cruelties in the provinces of the empire, designed to make the character of the emperor appear more despicable. Inciting her people to revolt, Bundovica says: "What shame and suffering have we not endured, since the Romans cast their eyes upon Britain. * * * Under Roman rule you cannot even die with impunity, for you know how they tax us even for the dead. Among other nations death frees even the slaves, but to the Romans even the dead live for their profit. * * * We have been humiliated and deceived by people who know nothing but to defraud."[10]

[1] Dio C. 62, 2.
[2] 62, 2.
[3] Plin. h. n. 5, 1, 14.
[4] Dio C. 62, 16.
[5] 62, 28.
[6] 63, 1-8.
[7] 63, 20-21.
[8] C. Jebb Greek Lit., p. 108.
[9] Dio C. 62, 3-5.
[10] 62, 3, seq.

And in her prayer to Andraste,[1] Bundovica is then quoted describing Nero as an effeminate ruling a nation of effeminate men. Now Tacitus has recorded numerous processes for extortion in the reign of Nero, stating the year in which they took place. The fact that these cases were so numerous prove two things, that the provinces still suffered from the injustice of governors, though some of the accused were acquitted, but that, on the other hand, under Nero the provinces were encouraged to complain.[2] And as to the effeminacy of the Romans, it is apparent that in this respect too the speech is nothing more than a brilliant piece of oratory. Tacitus too records a speech by Boadicea, as he calls her, said to have been addressed to her troops before the decisive battle, in which, though the extreme cruelties the Britains had suffered are mentioned, nothing is said about Roman effeminacy.[3] Dio needed a strong contrast to bring out the manly and heroic character of the British amazon.

The speech recorded as that of Vindex to the Gauls[4] is different. Its statements are borne out by the facts recorded elsewhere. It almost seems as though it had not been invented; it might at least have been held. Likewise the speeches of Nero and Tiridates at the coronation of the latter[5] may be assumed to have been held and recorded as held. Not only the circumstances render this probable, but it is also indicated by the fact that they are so brief, while the event is described at length. Most of the speeches, however, are of little value.

Dio is also fond of recording *prodigia*. He both begins and concludes the history of Nero by relating prodigies.[6] Those which were supposed to have occurred when Nero attempted to cut through the Isthmus of Corinth were of some historical interest, as they affected the undertaking.[7] But as a rule, Dio, unlike Tacitus, has no such interest in relating matters of this sort, but is again prompted by a desire to entertain.[8]

Sandys speaks of "the Roman annalists and other writers who uncritically transcribed, or rhetorically adorned the work of their predecessors."[9] Dio, though not exactly of the former, certainly belonged to the latter.

Dio claims chronological sequence for his presentation of events, but he frequently disregards this. Having related the death of Sabina (65 A. D.), he digresses on her beauty, and this

[1] 62, 6.
[2] Bury, Hist. of the Rom. Emp., p. 299.
[3] Ann. 14, 35.
[4] 63, 22.
[5] 63, 5.
[6] 62, 1; 63, 29.
[7] 63, 16.
[8] 61, 2, 4, 16, 1.
[9] Hist. of Class. Scholarsh., III, 236.

leads him to relate Nero's marriage to Sporos, who resembled Sabina. Here he adds, however, that this occurred later. As a rule, he fails to correct the false impression which he creates with regard to the sequence of events; and the reader must always be on his guard. We might ask whether this fault is to be attributed to Dio himself or to the abridgers of his work. In any definite statement regarding the date of an event or the duration of a period the abridger might be guilty of the error. Thus Xiphilinus and Zonaras disagree as to the length of Nero's life; Xiphilinus says that Nero lived 30 years and 9 months, Zonaras that he lived 30 years, 5 months, and 20 days.[1] But whenever the order of events is not correctly indicated, this must be attributed to Dio himself, both on account of the method of the abridgers and the positive disregard of chronology which appears from the unabridged parts of Dio's work.[2] It is Dio's way to bring together incidents in no wise connected, when they serve to illustrate.[3] The orgies arranged by Tigellinus and the burning of Rome (64 A. D.) he puts before the Eastern campaign of the year 63 A. D., because he wants to connect the former events with incidents of the year 63, such as the divorce of Octavia and the marriage of Sabina.[4]

It is also a fault of Dio that he attributes motives of which he has no proof. Regarding the burning of Rome, he says that Nero wanted to play the role of Priam outliving the destruction of his city.[5] When after the conflagration the emperor levied heavy taxes upon the empire, the rebuilding of Rome was only a pretext, the real motive being that he wanted funds to satisfy his extravagance.[6] While Tacitus, as a rule, mentions several possible motives, Dio does not hesitate to assign a definite motive.

Finally, it is peculiar to Dio's mode of treatment that, before relating the history of an emperor in detail, he gives *a brief sketch of his character and reign*. We have this biographical part preceding the annalistic also in the history of Nero.[7] It is a fault "to delineate the entire character at the very beginning and at once to emphasize or accentuate those traits which are sympathetic to the writer, or those which he dislikes or condemns. Thus does literary ambition or a certain predilection or prejudice over and over interfere with impartial historiography, and the slower and more patient study of the career

[1] Dio C. 63, 29. Zonaras 11, 13.
[2] Cp. Dio C. 37, 37. Sihler, Cic. of Arp., p. 169.
[3] 57, 17.
[4] 62, 16 sq.
[5] 62, 16.
[6] 62, 18.
[7] 61, 1-5.

and unfolding of an extraordinary personality becomes quite impossible."[1] The judgments and deductions with which these introductory sketches of Dio abound must therefore be taken with great care.

Characterization of Nero

Tacitus does not spare dark colors in his portrait of Nero, but has something to offset them; Suetonius is careful not to omit anything in his catalogue of the vicious and shameful deeds of the emperor, without giving due consideration to that which was good in his character and career; Dio exceeds both: he makes a display of the evil. He records every detail of Nero's nocturnal excesses in the streets of Rome;[2] he would lead the reader to believe that the incest between Nero and his mother was not only attempted;[3] the orgies arranged by Tigellinus are minutely described;[4] all the disgustingly immoral relations of Nero to women and men alike, and all the loathful perversity of his nature are brought out with great care;[5] the theatrical activities of the emperor of Rome could not be made to appear more despicable.[6]

But however much the picture of Nero in these respects may be overdrawn, Dio has succeeded in bringing out the dominating trait in this complicated character: his vanity. By indulging this fault of his nature in the early part of his reign the senate promoted the development of his other evil qualities;[7] the extravagance of the prince was owing partly to a desire to appear to be liberal;[8] to behold the beauty of the mother who bore Nero, he uncovered her breathless body;[9] that he might be admired and applauded, he degraded men and women of the aristocracy by having them appear with him in the theatre and the circus,[10] organized an army of claquers and even used coercive measures;[11] Bundovica tauntingly says that the Romans are serving a lyre-player, and a bad one at that;[12] his motive for setting fire to Rome is the desire to play the role of Priam;[13] planning to write a history of Rome, he would have it consist of 400 books, and banishes the learned Annaeus Cornutus for suggesting a smaller number;[14] he forbids Lucan to continue his literary activity, be-

[1] Sihler, Cic. of Arp., Introd., p. 7.
[2] Dio C. 61, 9.
[3] 61, 11. 12.
[4] 62, 15.
[5] 61, 12. 28; 63, 13.
[6] 61, 20.
[7] 61, 11.
[8] 61, 5.
[9] 61, 14.
[10] 61, 17.
[11] 61, 20.
[12] 62, 6.
[13] 62, 16.
[14] 62, 29.

cause his poems are lauded so highly;[1] his tour through Greece and his triumph after his return, of which there is a long and detailed description, show the emperor's highest ambition: to be acclaimed an Achilles and an Apollo;[2] when Nero finally saw himself deserted by all, he planned to kill all the senators, to burn the imperial city, and to sail to Alexandria, thinking that, if he lost his power, his "little art" would support him there;[3] and the last utterance of Nero which Dio records is the exclamation: "O Zeus, what an artist is perishing in me!"[4]

It is *Nero, the vain,* rather than the cruel and licentious, whom Dio describes; that vanity was one of the dominating traits of Nero's character, is confirmed by Suetonius, who emphasizes it together with his sensuality, and in Tacitus there is nothing to disprove the predominance of this trait. May we then not, while allowing for exaggeration, on the whole accept Dio's characterization of Nero as correct?

Resumé

What then is the value of Dio's history as far as Nero's life and reign are concerned? Dio's work is based on actual research with the use of original documents and of the works of various predecessors. But he is not thorough, his statements are often inaccurate and his judgments ill-supported, and he is guided too much by a desire to be entertaining, which influences his choice of material and misleads him to exaggerate, to invent motives, and to disregard the sequence of events. This desire to entertain the reader, as well as his hatred of the imperial tyrant, also makes him overdraw the character of Nero, but on the whole his characterization of the emperor is true. The value of Dio's Life of Nero then lies chiefly in supplying information, which other sources do not give us; it supplements to some extent Tacitus, and to a greater extent Suetonius.

Result

Of the works of the many who have written the history of Nero, "some of whom," according to Josephus, "have departed from the truth of facts, out of favor, as having received benefits from him, while others, out of hatred to him and the great ill-will which they bare him, have so impudently raved against him with their lies that they justly deserved to be condemned,"[5] we

[1] 62, 29.
[2] 63, 8-21.
[3] 63, 27.
[4] 63, 29.
[5] Antiq. 20, 8, 2.

possess only a few; and if these were to be numbered with either of the two classes named, or their successors, it should be the latter. But we can not class them with either, in spite of the faults that we have found.

Not only the Annals of Tacitus, but also the Life of Nero by Suetonius, and even the History of Nero by Dio Cassius are based on actual research. All three have compared a number of sources, and among these were some original documents.

But the three historians were not equally thorough and careful in their research nor equally faithful in recording the truth. In both respects Tacitus ranks much higher than Suetonius and Dio Cassius, and must therefore be preferred to them where they disagree with him, except in such instances in which it is quite evident that he has erred.[1]

Although the character and life of Nero, as well as his reign, would no doubt appear in a somewhat more favorable light, if he had his Velleius, as Tiberius has, or if the historical writings of Claudius, the Memoirs of Agrippina, and similar records had been preserved, yet the history of Nero, in the main, rests upon a fairly safe basis.

A few statements of the historians are placed beyond doubt by the testimony of inscriptions and coins.

Inscriptions

When Nero was declared an enemy of the state, this act of the senate was combined with a "damnatio memoriae." Accordingly the official records in marble and bronze, of which there must have been many, were ordered destroyed, or if they were not to be destroyed entirely, the removal of the hated tyrant's name from the inscriptions was demanded. The result is that very few inscriptions remain, and still fewer remain intact. These are, of course precious, while the value of the nameless inscriptions that seem to belong to Nero's reign is more or less doubtful.

We have already referred to the votive inscription to Nero which was found at Marquesia in Lusitania as showing the extent of the Neronian persecution of the Christians.[2]

An inscription that is dedicated to Nero as a flamen of the deified Augustus by his fellow members of the college of Augustan priests shows that it was part of the emperor's policy

[1] Hermann Schiller, Geschichte d. roem. Kaiserreiches unter d. Nero, p. 22-23.
[2] See p. 15. Gruteri Inscr. 238, 9.

to emphasize his relation to Augustus, an effectual means of securing to himself the attachment of the Guard.[1]

Coins

Since the year 44 B. C., a short time before Caesar's death, Roman coins became documents of the imperial history of Rome. For then the senate passed a resolution to replace the head of the god which theretofore Roman coins had borne on their face by the head of the dictator. The right of coinage, which in accord with custom, was exercised by generals in their provinces, Caesar had already assumed also in the capitol.[2] The senate, however, had also enjoyed that right, and continued to do so even under Augustus. In 15 B. C. a definite arrangement was adopted whereby the emperor reserved to himself the right of coining gold and silver, and left to the senate only the coining of copper. This circumstance indicated the change that had taken place in the form of government. The republic had been converted into a monarchy.[3] After the year 11 B. C. the names of the directors of the mint (triumviri monetales) no longer appear on the extant coins, the last name being that of C. Sulpicius Platorinus, which is found on a coin with the head of Agrippa, who died in that year.[4] From this time on the face of every Roman coin presents the picture of an emperor or of some member of his family, while the reverse side is a memorial of some achievement of his or some act of benevolence bestowed by him.[5] From this time on then the coins become in a greater measure records of imperial history.

Not a few of the extant coins belong to the reign of Nero. In connection with the literary sources, these coins form a valuable kind of evidence, notwithstanding the autobiographical nature of the data they furnish.

Thus a number of coins throw light upon Agrippina's relation to Nero and to the imperial government during the early part of his reign. When the Parthians arose in 54 A. D. the people, says Tacitus, asked what dependence the state could repose in a man *governed by a woman*.[6] Tacitus also tells us how through Nero the mother controlled the senate; that at the instigation of Agrippina the senate was called to meet in the palace, where, concealed behind portieres, she could overhear the discussions.

---

[1] Gruteri Inscr., 237, 1: NERONI CAESARI GERMANI F. TIB. AUGUSTI N. DIVI. AUG. PRON. FLAMINI AUGUSTALI. Cp. Suet. Nero 7; Tac. Ann. 13, 19; 14, 7.
[2] Mommsen, Roem. Muenzwesen, p. 729 seq.; cp. Eckhel.
[3] Mommsen, Ueber d. roem. Muenzwesen, I. 1.
[4] Eckhel, p. 123.
[5] Peter, Die geschichtl. Lt., I, 259.
[6] Ann. 13, 6.

and that she openly opposed some measures.[1] He shows to what extent Agrippina had assumed control of foreign affairs by relating that at the reception of the Armenian embassy in 54 A. D., she attempted to ascend the imperial tribunal and to preside jointly with the emperor, an attempt that was frustrated only by the prudence of Seneca.[2] Dio says that in the beginning of Nero's reign Agrippina conducted all the affairs of the government for him[3] and in his name.[4] The records of the coins very strongly confirm these statements.

Two coins from the early part of Nero's reign are described by Eckhel as follows:[5]

AGRIPP. AUG. DIVI. CLAUD. NERONIS. CAES. MATER.
Capita adversa Neronis nudum, et Agrippinae.
NERONI. CLAUD. DIVI. F. CAES, AUG. GERM. IMP. TR. P.
Corona querna, inter quam
EX. S. C. AV. AR.

NERO. CLAUD. DIVI. F. CAES. AUG. GERM. IMP. TR. P. COS.
Capita jugata Neronis nudum, et Agrippinae.
AGRIPP. AUG. DIVI. CLAUD. NERONIS. CAES. MATER. EX. S. C.
Duae figurae, quarum dexterior aquilam legionariam, altera hastam, et pateram tenet, sedentes in quadrigis elephantorum.
AV. AR.

The picture and name of an empress on Roman coins was nothing new. There are coins which bear Livia's title and image;[6] but these are not among the imperial coins.[7] As far as the extant Roman coins show, none bore the image of any of Nero's wives, not even that of Poppaea Sabina.[8] Agrippina was the first woman whose head appeared on imperial coins along with that of the Princeps, first with that of Claudius,[9] and then with that of Nero.

It is noteworthy that all of the coins that are symbolic of her co-regency are imperial coins, while the senate, it seems, did not issue such coins.[10] This circumstance already indicates the opposition of the senate, which was united with Seneca and Burrus, the counselors of the Princeps, whose influence, however, as yet was not sufficient to warrant any open interference with Agrippina's acts. They had to suffer for a while that "she behaved as the regent of the empire."[11]

[1] Ann. 13, 6.
[2] Ann. 13, 5. Dio C. 61, 3.
[3] Dio C. 61, 3.
[4] Zonaras 11, 12.
[5] Eckhel, p. 262.
[6] Eckhel, p. 149.
[7] Eckhel, p. 148: Commatis Romani numus vivo marito signatus non extat.
[8] Eckhel, p. 285.
[9] Eckhel, p. 257.
[10] Schiller, Gesch. d. roem. Kaisers. 1, 344.
[11] Bury, History of the Rom. Emp., p. 275.

It was not until Agrippina had lost her influence over Nero that Seneca and Burrus put an end to her rule. The love affair with Acte, the dismissal of Pallas, Agrippina's adulterer and political consort, from his office as treasurer, Agrippina's threat to espouse the cause of Britannicus, and his resulting death early in the year 55, mark the removal of Agrippina from participation in the government. From Tacitus alone[1] we learn the time of this important change. But the coins confirm his statements. The first of the two coins described was issued soon after Nero's accession, before he entered upon his first consulate. The second is of the year 55, for it designates Nero as consul, and this was the year of his first consulship. The coin shows that at the beginning of 55 Agrippina's influence was still strong. But on a coin recording Nero's second tribunate (55 A. D.),[2] and on another recording his third tribunate (56 A. D.),[3] the mother's image and inscription is not found, nor is it found on any later coin. Seneca and Burrus are now administering the affairs of the empire.

Greek and Egyptian coins commemorating Nero's "victories" on his tour in Greece are testimonies to his vanity, perpetuating the memory of "NERO APOLLO."[4]

---

[1] Ann. 13, 14, seq.
[2] Tac. Ann. 13, 11.
[3] Eckhel, p. 262.
[4] Eckhel, p. 276.

Bibliography

In the following list only those works are mentioned which the writer in the limited time that was at his disposal could actually use. A comprehensive list of works on the subject will be found in Henderson's "Life and Principate of the Emperor Nero."

I—Source Books.

Cornelii Taciti Libri qui supersunt, ed. Carolus Halm. Leipzig, Teubner, 1912.

C. Suetoni Tranquilli quae supersunt omnia, rec. Carolus Ludovicus Roth. Leipzig, Teubner, 1871.

Hermann Peter, Historicorum Romanorum Fragmenta. Leipzig, Teubner, 1883.

C. Plinii Caecili Secundi, epistularum libri novem, epistularum ad Traianum liber, Panegyricus, ed. H. Keil. Leipzig, Teubner, 1853.

Dionis Cassii Cocceiani historia Romana, ed. Ludovicus Dindorfius. Leipzig, Teubner, 1864.

Ioannis Zonarae epitome historiarum, vol. III., ed. Ludovicus Dindorfius. Leipzig, 1870.

Pauli Orosii adversus paganos historiarum libri VII.

Flavi Josephi opera omnia, ed. Immanuel Bekker. Leipzig, 1856. Vol. III.

Eusebii Pamphili historiae ecclesiasticae libri X, ed. F. A. Heinichen. Leipzig, C. G. Kayser, 1827.

Iani Gruteri, inscriptiones antiquae totius orbis Romani.

Joseph Eckhel, Doctrina Numorum Veterum, Pars II., Vol. VI. Vindobonae, 1796.

II—Works on the Sources and Other Works.

Karl Nipperdey, Cornelius Tacitus. Berlin, Weidmannsche Buchhandlung, 1871.

G. A. Ruperti, C. C. Taciti Opera. Hannover, 1834.

A. Draeger, Ueber Syntax und Stil des Tacitus. Leipzig, 1882.

Jan Bergmans, Die Quellen der Vita Tiberii des Cassius Dio. Amsterdam, Hoeveker und Wormser, 1903.

O. Clason, Tacitus und Sueton, Breslau, 1870.

Hermann, Peter, Die geschichtliche Litteratur ueber die roemische Kaiserzeit bis Theodosius I. Leipzig, Teubner, 1897.

G. Boissier, Tacite. Paris, Librairie Hachette Et Cie, 1903.

Henry Fynes Clinton, Fasti Romani. Oxford, University Press, 1845.

John Edwin Sandys, A History of Classical Scholarship. Second Edition. Cambridge, University Press, 1906.

John Edwin Sandys, A Companion to Latin Studies. Cambridge, University Press, 1910.

Pauly, Realencyclopaedie der klassischen Altertumswissenschaft. Stuttgart, 1846.

Pauly-Wissowa, Realencyclopaedie der klassischen Altertumswissenschaft, 1899-1900.

Teuffel and Schwabe, History of Roman Literature. London, George Bell & Sons, 1891.

A. S. Wilkins, Roman Literature. London, MacMillan, 1914.

Theodor Mommsen, Roemisches Muenzwesen. Berlin, Weidmannsche Buchh., 1860.

Theodor Mommsen, Ueber das roem. Muenzwesen. Kleine schriften aus d. Abhandlungen d. k. saechsischen Gesellschaft der Wissenschaften, vol. II.

Ed. Aug. Freeman, Methods of Historical Study. London, MacMillan, 1886.

E. G. Sihler, Cicero of Arpinum. New Haven, Yale University Press, 1914.

III—Modern Works on the History of Nero.

Hermann Schiller, Geschichte der roemischen Kaiserzeit Gotha, 1883.

Hermann Schiller, Geschichte des roemischen Kaiserreichs unter der Regierung des Nero. Berlin, Weidmannsche Buchhandlung, 1872.

B. W. Henderson, The Life and Principate of the Emperor Nero. London, Methuen & Co., 1903.

J. B. Bury, A History of the Roman Empire. American Book Co.

Charles Merivale, History of the Romans under the Empire. Fourth Ed. New York, Appleton, 1889.

H. F. Pelham, Outlines of Roman History. New York, Putnam, 1893.

Edw. Gibbon, History of the Decline and Fall of the Roman Empire. Philadelphia, Porter.

Samuel Dill, Roman Society from Nero to Marcus Aurelius. London, MacMillan, 1898.

W. M. Ramsay, The Church in the Roman Empire before A. D. 170. New York, Putnam, 1893.

Ludwig Friedlaender, Roman Life and Manners under the Early Empire. Authorized Translation of the Seventh Enlarged and Revised Edition of the Sittengeschichte Roms by L. A. Magnus. New York, E. P. Dutton & Co.

Printed by Libri Plureos GmbH in Hamburg, Germany